DAWN TO DUSK IN THE GALÁPAGOS

"DAWN TO DUSK IN"

Flightless Birds,

Swimming Lizards,

THE GALÁPAGOS

TEXT BY
RITA GOLDEN GELMAN

PHOTOGRAPHS BY
TUI DE ROY

Little, Brown and Company
Boston Toronto London

and Other Fascinating Creatures

First Edition

Library of Congress Cataloging-in-Publication Data

Gelman, Rita Golden.
    Dawn to dusk in the Galápagos: flightless birds,
swimming lizards, and other fascinating creatures /
text by Rita Golden Gelman; photographs by Tui De
Roy. — 1st ed.
        p.   cm.
    Summary: Text and photographs explore the vast
array of unusual creatures still to be found in the
Galápagos Islands.
    ISBN 0-316-30739-4
    1. Zoology — Galápagos Islands — Juvenile liter-
ature. [1. Zoology — Galápagos Islands.] I. De
Roy, Tui, ill. II. Title.
QL 345. G2G45 1991
591.9866'5 — dc20   90-6281

        10 9 8 7 6 5 4 3 2 1

                    WOR

        Published simultaneously in Canada
    by Little, Brown & Company (Canada) Limited

        Printed in the United States of America

At first, there was ocean, miles and miles of ocean. No land. Just wind and waves.

Then the hot center of the earth burst through the ocean bottom and red molten lava shot through the water. Over and over again it happened. The ocean boiled. Lava piled on top of lava. And slowly, but violently, over millions of years, mountains grew under the water.

Four or five million years ago, some of those mountains reached the air . . . and the Galápagos Islands were born.

They were islands without plants. Without animals. Just hard black lava.

Then life arrived.

It came in the form of sea birds that discovered the new islands when they flew over them. And it came in the form of seeds, carried in the wind, or stuck on the feet of birds, matted in their feathers, deposited in their droppings.

There must have been thousands of seeds before one of them landed in a place where the lava was crumbly enough for a plant to take root. And perhaps there were thousands of those tiny plants before one of them was tough enough to withstand the blistering sun and the dry conditions.

But there was no hurry. Over thousands of years, some of the islands began to look green. Then, not only sea birds but land birds could find food on the islands.

Other animals arrived. No one knows for sure how they got there. They couldn't swim and they couldn't fly. And the nearest land was the coast of Ecuador, six hundred miles away.

Most of them probably arrived on rafts of vegetation torn from the mainland by violent storms and washed out into the ocean. Those rafts, among millions bobbing in the sea, happened to bump into the Galápagos Islands — and the animals got off.

Today the Galápagos consist of fourteen major islands and dozens of lava formations sticking up out of the water. The volcanoes continue to erupt; the islands continue to grow.

On some of the islands there are people, even small towns. In all, some ten thousand people live on four of the islands.

But the other islands belong to the animals, animals that have learned to share the food supply, the living space, the ocean.

People can visit during the daytime hours and walk among the animals, even swim with them off the shore. The animals of the Galápagos are not afraid of people. But the people cannot stay.

The islands belong to the animals.

The night sky is filled with stars and the tiniest sliver of a moon. Below, wave after wave after wave explodes into white foam against the cliffs, cliffs created by volcanoes, sculpted by the ocean and the winds.

Near the cliffs, in the spray of the waves, several big brown lumps — sea lions — are sprawled on the sand, sleeping. A female rolls onto her stomach and her pup squeals for a nipple. The wriggling pup bumps into the pup next to him.

A series of squeals. All the lumps twist, wriggle, stretch, snort, and go back to sleep. A sneeze. A cough.

Then, from the big bull in the corner, come ten long grunts that sound like giant burps. Even in the night, the bull is protecting the females and pups. He wants no intruder in his territory, no wandering bull that might be looking for a place to sleep or a territory to steal. So all night long, every half hour or so, he grunts out his warning.

He can be heard a mile away, where blue-footed boobies are sleeping, their heads tucked under loose wing feathers. The booby colony is quiet except for the occasional slap, slap, slap of big blue feet, shaking off mosquitoes.

And he can be heard in the frigate camp, where the big black birds that soar and dive and rob by day are motionless by night, sleeping in their bushtop nests.

Only a few feet from the bull, on a slab of lava that hangs over the ocean, marine iguanas are piled up in a big black mound. The only sound from the pile is a wet sneeze now and then. Iguanas swallow a lot of salt water, and they have a special gland that lets them squirt out most of the salt through their nostrils in a sort of spit-sneeze.

There are other iguanas: in the cracks, under rocks, in little lava caves. They are hiding from the cool night air.

Circling in the darkness above the sea lions and iguanas are eight swallow-tailed gulls. Some are on their way out to look for food. Others are on their way back, stuffed with fish and squid to feed their chicks. The air is filled with the strange squeaky noises and clicking sounds of the returning adults.

One baby swallow-tailed gull, waiting on a ledge, recognizes his mother's call. He shrieks again and again. In the dark the mother flies toward her chick's call. She lowers her little red feet, raises her wings, and lands.

Immediately the chick begins pecking at the white patch on his mother's beak. She leans forward and opens her mouth. The chick opens his beak and receives the partially digested fish his mother brings up from inside.

Galápagos swallow-tailed gulls are the only night gulls in the world. They have big red-rimmed eyes that glow in the dark and give them special night vision. They also have a white spot on their beak that helps their chicks feed in the dark.

The gulls that first came to the Galápagos several million years ago had black beaks, "day eyes," and they slept at night. But in the Galápagos they ran into frigate birds. Frigates steal food from gulls by pestering them until they throw it up. Then the frigates catch it in midair and fly off.

When the gulls first encountered frigates, some of them, in desperation, must have tried to go out at night while the frigates were sleeping. But their eyes were not made for night fishing. It must have been difficult, too, for them to find their nests in the dark.

But, purely by chance, some gulls had better night vision than others. They were the ones that caught the most fish and made it back to their nests in the dark. Their chicks, chicks that inherited the good eyesight of their parents, were well fed and healthy. And they, in turn, had the healthiest chicks. Over many thousands of years, the gulls with the best eyesight continued to have the healthiest chicks. At the same time, the gulls with poor night vision couldn't get enough food and they began dying out . . . until, after thousands and thousands of years, all the Galápagos swallow-tailed gulls had "night eyes." The white patches on their beaks developed in the same way.

This kind of change in the way animals look and behave in order to survive is called evolution. And it's why, in the middle of the night, dozens of swallow-tailed parents are able to feed their chicks in peace.

Meanwhile, on a small beach on a different island, in the light of the stars, seven marine turtles have come out of the water to lay their eggs.

They are flinging the sand with their front flippers. One kicks, then another, then all of them are kicking, and the small beach is caught in a sandstorm.

One turtle has finished digging a pit big enough to fit her body. Now she carefully shapes the small hole where she will lay her eggs. She will lay between seventy and one hundred eggs. When she is finished, she will cover the eggs with sand, climb out of the pit, and return to the water, leaving a trail behind her.

She will be far away when the eggs hatch and the tiny turtles try to make it into the water before the crabs or frigates or mockingbirds get them. Only a small number of the hatchlings will survive to become adults. But it is enough to keep the species healthy.

As night begins to turn into day, the marine iguanas come out from their sleeping places. One by one, black like the lava and cold from the night, they stretch on the rocks so every bit of their skin can soak up the warmth of the rising sun.

On another island, high up in a crater at the top of a volcanic mountain, giant tortoises are also waking up. Some have slept under bushes, in "beds" scooped out of the ground.

Now they make their way slowly out into the sun.

By the time the tortoises are in the sun, most of the sea lions have had their first swim. On one rocky shore, a female has stayed behind to care for her newborn pup, just minutes old. The mother and pup rub noses, squiggle their bodies against each other, and call back and forth. The pup sounds like a lamb bleating; the mother's voice is deeper, like a sheep's.

In the middle of the island, spread out over the dry, dusty dirt, the blue-footed boobies are starting their day . . . wing-stretching, neck-twisting, opening their six-inch beaks in yawns. The males are whistling. The females are honking. The chicks are calling for food with a soft clucking sound, almost like rapid hiccups.

Many of the adults are waterproofing themselves, twisting their necks around to rub the oil sacks at the base of their tails and then spreading oil on every "hair" of every feather.

Other adult boobies have already gone out diving. About half a mile offshore, nine boobies fly together over the ocean, their eyes fixed on the water.

Suddenly there is a whistle, other whistles, honks.

The ocean below is boiling with jumping fish, thousands of them, leaping out of the water, trying to escape from a school of hungry tuna.

The boobies dive-bomb from fifty feet up. By the time the first group is back up and ready to dive again, dozens more have arrived. Thirty, forty, sixty boobies honking, whistling, flapping, diving.

Two frigates go after a booby, pulling on her tail. The booby screeches out a distress call. She twists; she wriggles. The frigates grab her wings and shake her. Finally, the booby regurgitates the fish. As the fish falls toward the water, one of the frigates makes a sharp turn, angles in, dives down . . . and catches the fish in midair.

Frigates are very agile in the air. They use their long forked tails to steer into sharp turns. They change direction in a fraction of a second. They soar on the wind currents for hours without flapping their giant wings.

But they have trouble getting off the ground. Their huge wings, seven feet from tip to tip, need room to make the long downstroke that will lift them up and into flight. Frigates live on the tops of bushes or trees, where it is easier to take off flapping, the air under their wings.

In the water, they have the same takeoff problems. And to make things worse, they are not very waterproof. Unlike those of other sea birds, frigate feathers can get waterlogged.

So the frigates try to get their meals without getting wet. Sometimes they catch flying fish as they leap out of the water; sometimes they snatch fish that are swimming near the top. And sometimes they steal their meals from other birds . . . such as boobies and gulls.

Frigates are called *cleptoparasites,* animals that live off other animals by stealing from them.

Trick flying, catching things in midair, poking and pestering other birds is skilled work. Back at the frigate colony, it is early morning, and many of the young birds are learning how to be frigates.

The very young chicks stand in their nests on the tops of bushes and trees, just staring into space. Every once in a while they open their wings, squawk, lose their balance, catch it, and then go back to staring into space. They are big, puffy, silly-looking chicks with nothing to do but bake in the sun and wait for a parent to come feed them.

Other youngsters, just a little older, practice flapping. They open their wings and wave them around awkwardly, sometimes knocking themselves over.

Five- and six-month-old frigates flap gracefully, slowly, as though they are flying. But they don't go anywhere. They just stand there in their trees, flapping, ten flaps, twenty flaps. Then they rest. They're still too young to fly, but they are building their muscles. One day soon, they'll flap their wings, jump from their bushtop nests, and fly. Then they'll be ready to practice their other skills.

Three frigate juveniles chase each other in the air over the colony. One of them is carrying a stick. He drops it. The other two go after the stick; both miss, and the stick drops to the ground. Again and again, the young frigates chase each other in the air and play with sticks, trying to catch them the way they will one day have to catch flying fish or the food they rob from boobies and gulls. These juveniles are nearly a year and a half old. Very soon their parents will stop feeding them, and they will be on their own. If they learn their lessons well, they will be able to eat.

By midmorning, the reptiles have warmed up.

Giant tortoises slowly make their way along "tortoise highways," paths that have been used by tortoises for thousands of years. As they move, the vegetation is crushed beneath them and their "shells," called carapaces, clunk on the lava rocks.

One tortoise, a male, is chewing on some grass. A tiny finch hops up and down in front of the tortoise's face. And he keeps hopping until the tortoise notices him.

When the tortoise sees the finch, he stops eating and reaches his neck way up. He stands tall on his feet, stretching out the folds of skin on his crinkly, fat legs.

And then, he waits.

The finch hops onto the tortoise's head and pokes its beak around the big animal's eyes, picking out the tiny ticks that have embedded themselves in the tortoise's skin. Then the bird hops onto one of the legs and pokes around some more. The tortoise stands absolutely still as the finch pokes and picks at his skin.

The finch and the tortoise are helping each other. The tortoise is getting rid of bothersome ticks. And the finch is getting a meal.

Not far from the tortoises, a little lava lizard has already had a successful morning; a half-eaten grasshopper is sticking out of his mouth.

On the other side of the crater, a land iguana, larger and fatter than his marine cousins, scrapes the spines off a cactus leaf with the claws and pad of his leathery foot, and then, with what looks like a perpetually smiling mouth, he begins to eat.

Back on the shore, the marine iguanas munch on algae covering the wet lava rocks. The smallest iguanas squeeze into the cracks. Big females press their flattish noses into the algae on the outer surfaces of the rocks. Sally Light-foot crabs decorate the black lava with their bright shells as they, too, scavenge for algae. Only the big male iguanas are still sunning, waiting until midday, when they will go into the water to dive for their food.

On the southernmost island, thousands of waved albatrosses are sitting in the rising sun, tending eggs, shading chicks, staring blankly into space.

One father rolls his egg along the ground with his beak. Albatrosses don't make real nests. They just roll their eggs to a new place every now and then.

Some of the egg caretakers have been sitting with their eggs for more than two weeks straight, with no trips out to sea to eat. Soon their mates will come to relieve them. But for now, they sit, hungry and losing weight.

As the sun angles its way up, one lone albatross returns from a feeding trip. Instead of gently floating in, he lands hard and topples over. Briefly stunned, but not injured, he gets up and immediately begins calling out a low, one-note song.

Soon there is a gurgly squeal from the "chick nursery" under a bush, where seven young albatrosses are waiting for their parents. A funny brown chick waddles awkwardly out from his bush, calling again and again. Back and forth they call and waddle, until finally they find each other.

The hungry chick begins pecking at the base of the father's beak, squealing for food. The father lowers his head and opens his beak. The chick puts his beak inside the father's and rubs the back of his father's tongue to stimulate regurgitation.

The food that the father has eaten during his two-week fishing trip has been converted into oil. From the opening in the back of his throat, the father squirts the oil into the chick's throat, pumping and grunting to get the oil up and out. Then he stops and the chick swallows, dribbling fishy-smelling oil down his body. When he is

full, the chick has enough oil to nourish his body for a couple of weeks. His stomach is bulging; his downy covering is sticky and smelly. He has been turned into a big oil-filled skin, so heavy that he can hardly stand. At five months old, the chick weighs nearly twice as much as his parent. As he waddles back to his bush, he walks on the lower part of his legs, too unbalanced with all that oil sloshing around inside to walk only on his feet.

Meanwhile, the boobies are dancing. One male lifts his big blue feet, first one, then the other; then he points his beak at the sky, raises his wings, and whistles. The female, bigger than the male, lifts her feet, too, and calls out in her deeper, louder voice. They touch beaks and necks. They ruffle their wings, flutter their feathers.

After a ten-minute dance, the male booby takes off and flies in a circle. Then he lands, pushing his feet way out in front of his body, showing them off. He whistles. She honks.

Then he picks up a stick and gives it to her.

She places it on the dirt. Then she moves it to another spot. Then another. He walks away and brings back a pebble. She places it next to the stick. They are deciding where to lay their eggs and brood their chicks.

A father nearby is guarding two eggs. His blue feet are wrapped around them, protecting them from the sun.

Just across the way a mother is shading her chick by putting her body between the sun and the chick. All day long she stands there, turning as the sun crosses the sky. They are surrounded by a white circle of bird droppings, squirted out by the adult as she turns with the sun.

As the heat intensifies, the blue-footed boobies become quiet and still. Hundreds of them stand unprotected in the sun, panting to cool off and holding their wings away from their bodies so the breezes can blow through them.

Boobies with eggs or chicks cannot retreat into the shade. If they leave, the burning sun will kill their chicks and dry up their eggs.

Not far away, there is a colony of masked boobies. They are different from the blue-footed boobies, in both looks and behavior.

Blue-footed boobies often have two or three chicks. They dive for their food close to shore, and in the course of the day they can fly back and forth to their nests to feed their chicks.

Masked boobies feed way out in the ocean. They usually raise only one chick because they cannot fly back often enough to feed more than one. It's probable that if the parents had to take care of two chicks, neither one would survive.

Yet masked boobies always lay two eggs, just in case the first one breaks, gets eaten, or doesn't hatch.

Now, in the heat of midday, a mother masked booby is shading her five-day-old chick while the second egg, tucked underneath one of her webbed feet, is hatching. The egg cracks under the mother's foot and a tiny helpless pink thing wriggles out of the shell. The older chick, like other first-born masked boobies, nudges the newborn away from the parent's protection, out into the sun. The delicate, unprotected newborn will not survive ten minutes.

All over the masked booby colony, where there are chicks, there are dried bodies of the second-born chicks.

In the early afternoon hours, the sun is at its hottest. The bushes and grasses and boulders writhe in the distortions of the rising heat.

The giant Galápagos tortoises are sound asleep. Some have wriggled into their shaded "beds"; others stay cool in ponds.

The land iguanas are hiding in their burrows and under bushes. If they get too hot, their bodies will stop functioning.

At the shore, the marine iguanas are also in danger of overheating. Many of the females and the young have returned to the shaded rocks and crevices for a few hours. Others are lined up on the rocks, facing the sun with their heads high, holding their chests off the hot rocks, and shading as much of their bodies as they can.

Many of the male marine iguanas are in the water. One big male walks straight down a small cliff, his sharp claws digging into the air-bubble holes in the rocks. When he reaches the water, he slips in, tucks his feet against his sides, and begins to move his tail from side to side like a flexible paddle. He dives deep and stays under for nearly half an hour, munching on the algae at the bottom, moving from spot to spot by waving his tail.

The Galápagos marine iguanas are the only iguanas in the world that swim and dive for their food. Once upon a time, their ancestors lived off the land, like other lizards. They got their food from the trees or from the ground. They had rounder tails, lighter skin, pointier noses. They did just fine until they found themselves in a world where there wasn't enough to eat on land.

The iguanas that were able to change their diet and eat algae were able to find food. The ones that just happened to have flatter tails could swim better and get to the algae that were under the water. And the ones that had flatter noses found it easier to eat the algae that were growing out of the rocks. Some were fortunate enough to be darker in color; they heated up faster in the sun, and they could spend more time in the cold water, getting food.

The healthiest, strongest iguanas had the most and the healthiest babies, many of which were born with their parents' special abilities. They, too, had the most, the healthiest, and the strongest children. And, over hundreds of thousands of years, the iguanas changed, until all of them ate algae, had flatter tails, blunter noses, and darker skin. They had evolved into a new type of iguana — the marine iguana.

Meanwhile, on powdery white beaches with sand of coral, on purple beaches of sea urchin spines, on black beaches, green beaches, red beaches . . . on smooth slabs of lava, on jagged stones, in caves, under bushes, in tidal pools, in furious surf, in gently flowing waves, are the ubiquitous sea lions.

Some are bodysurfing. Others are "porpoising" in and out of the water. One sea lion is chasing an iguana under the water. Another is lying on her side, holding her front fin like a sail.

Just off one beach a bull is on patrol, barking every few minutes. He is watching the young ones, scolding them if they go out too far. From time to time sharks swim in, looking for young sea lions; the bull places himself between the pups and the sharks.

The bull has been patrolling his territory for nearly two weeks. He has barely slept. He has not gone out to feed . . . although now and then he swallowed a fish that came by.

All day long the bull swims back and forth, watching, guarding, calling out his warning. And often he patrols at night as well.

Very soon another bull will challenge him. And the resident bull will probably lose. He is weak and tired. He will leave his territory and go out to feed. He may live for a while in a bachelor colony where there are only bulls . . . bulls without territories. Then, one day, he will challenge someone, maybe even the bull that challenged him. And perhaps he will again have a territory.

Meanwhile, the pup that was born a few hours ago is about to get his first swimming lesson. His mother is nudging him over the rocks. He is squirming, squeaking, crying out in protest as he stumbles, gets caught in the cracks, steps on the sharp edges of the lava. His mother keeps pulling him out of trouble, helping him over rough spots.

Finally, she picks him up by his neck and carries him into the water. He wails and squirms. She pushes him back and forth. They are in the water for less than five minutes. Then she picks him up again and carries him back to shore. He nuzzles in close and begins sucking on her nipple.

Nearby, an older pup waddles into the water and calls for his mother. She is on the other side of the rocks, but she recognizes his voice. She calls back. He hears her and begins swimming toward the sound.

Other pups are playing. One is playing with a yellow leaf. Another is playing with the tail of a basking iguana. She pokes it. She pushes it. She nibbles on it. The iguana moves to another spot. The pup leaves the iguana and begins chasing a crab. The crab runs into a crack between two rocks. The pup finds a sea lion friend. She bites his flipper. She nibbles on his nose. The friend nibbles back. They open up their very pink mouths and growl and whine at each other, play-biting. Then they both lie down, their bodies tucked into each other, their whiskers intertwined. The female tosses her fin across her friend and closes her eyes.

As the sun moves lower in the sky, a small finch is poking her long thin beak into a flower.

On another island, a finch is cracking a seed with his fat powerful beak.

And still another finch on another island is holding a cactus spine in her medium-sized beak and poking it into a hole in a tree. There is a wormlike larva in the hole, and the finch is hoping to have it for supper.

When finches first arrived in the Galápagos, their beaks were more or less the same. But over the years, the finches have become specialists, and their beaks, like the eyes of the swallow-tailed gulls and the tails of the iguanas, changed, favoring those variations that helped the finches get the food that was available. The finches in the Galápagos are another example of evolution.

In the late afternoon, the frigate colony pulses with strange yodeling noises, fluttery calls that are coming from male frigates with big red balloons under their beaks. Each male spent about half an hour inflating his balloon, which is usually a tiny pink skin flap hanging under his beak. It is one way he makes himself attractive to females.

A few minutes ago, the males were quiet in their puffed-up splendor. Then a female flew overhead. As soon as the males saw her, they went crazy, calling, shaking, wiggling their balloons, fluttering their wings, pointing their beaks at the sky.

They are all trying to woo the same female, the only female around at the moment.

She circles a few times until the males are frenzied. Then she lands next to one of them. He calls, throws his head back, shakes his wings. They rub their necks against each other. They wriggle their chests together. He surrounds her with his wings. Then they just stand there, staring straight ahead.

She stays for a few minutes, then flies off, creating new hope for other frigates. They begin to call and quiver all over again.

As the shadows get longer and the island begins to cool off, the marine iguanas once again cover the still-warm rocks with their sprawled bodies.

The adult boobies are returning from their fishing trips, and the colony is again filled with the honks of the females, the whistles of the males, and the hiccupy sound of the chicks begging for food.

On the albatross island, a young bird stands at the edge of a cliff, looking out at the water. Every once in a while, he leans forward and opens his wings, apparently about to take off. But each time, he changes his mind and folds up again.

Albatrosses have trouble taking off. When they are on the ground, they walk to the edge of a cliff and jump into the wind. When they are at sea, they wait for a big wave and run on top of it, flapping and kicking their legs. Once they are up, they can ride the wind for hours without moving their eight-foot wings.

Over and over the young albatross on the cliff seems to be about to take off. He leans forward, opens his wings . . . and closes them again. Finally, he waddles away from the cliff.

He passes a dancing couple. The male and female are calling to each other in a low wailing moan. They throw their heads back and point to the sky. Then they fence with their beaks.

Albatross couples stay together for life; and every year, when they lay their eggs and raise their chicks, they dance again.

On another island far to the west, a flightless cormorant is standing on a black lava rock; her useless raggedy wings are spread out to dry.

When cormorants first arrived in the Galápagos, one or two million years ago, their wings were full and strong. They were able to fly long distances to get food and they could escape from land predators by taking off into the air.

On their new island home they discovered that there were no land predators . . . and food was just offshore. They no longer needed to fly. Over many thousands of years, their wings gradually became tattered, their flying muscles weak. The Galápagos cormorants have even lost part of the bone where, in other cormorants, flight muscles are attached.

On the other side of the cormorant island, penguins are making the last dive of the day. Penguins, like cormorants, are birds that cannot fly. But penguins do use their wings to propel themselves in the water.

Thousands of years ago the penguins came to the Galápagos from the south. Somehow they managed to survive on the equator, making their homes on the cooler islands where a cold current washes the lava rocks.

The penguins are using their wings to paddle quietly along when suddenly they take off in all directions, arching their bodies in and out of the water at more than twenty miles per hour, diving with a powerful down-pull of their wings, steering with their webbed feet, coming up, diving again. They are after a school of fish. The chase continues, furiously, for three minutes. Then, the fish are gone.

When the dive is over, it is time for the penguins to feed their chicks, to oil their feathers, or to stand on the rocks and watch the sun set.

On a faraway shore, in the rocky cliffs, the swallow-tailed gulls are getting ready to go out for their night feeding. Some are combing and oiling their feathers. Others are circling.

Already the giant tortoises are sleeping.

The marine iguanas are in their nighttime mounds.

And the land iguanas are in their burrows.

Boobies are returning in groups — ten, twenty, thirty dark shadows against the orange sky. Soon they will tuck their heads under their wings and sleep.

The frigates, too, will soon be asleep in the tops of their trees.

As the sun disappears into the water, the bull sea lion grunts out his warning. The pups wriggle and squeal and nestle close to the warm bodies of their mothers.

The sky darkens.
The stars appear.
And the sliver moon is a little bit bigger.
And still, and forever, the ocean explodes into foam against the cliffs. Wave after wave after wave.